First and Last Lines:
Exercises for Writers and Students

Kristin Scarbrough

Creative Writing Flow Vol One

KScarbrough Publications
2013 Dry Fork Valley Rd
Philadelphia, TN 37846
www.kscarbrough.space

Introduction

The intention of this book is to provide writers and teachers of creative writing with exercises to help sharpen their skills; it is not an instructional book on writing. There is the assumption of some experience with writing or these exercises to be an accompaniment to instruction. If you are a teacher, you'll need a workbook for each student. The first section consists of sentences to be used as a first line in a short story or a brief paragraph. The second section consists of sentences to be used as last lines.

Some ideas for using the lines: Pick and choose which lines to use for practice. Go through the lines in order, recording all story attempts in a writing journal. Pick a line and write as many interpretations as you can of the same sentence. Switch the lines – use a first line as a last line or a last line as a first line. Try pairing up the lines, one first line and one last line, especially ones that don't seem to match. Take any of the lines and use them in the middle of your story. The most important thing to remember when using these exercises is to have fun!

First Lines

It was just one kiss but everything quickly went wrong.

He normally went to the gym after work, but today was different.

The laundry wasn't going to do itself.

She did her best to resist, but she desperately wanted to know what was in the box.

From some reason, the sock was purple.

He was positive he'd left his wallet at work.

The cat was yowling at the door again.

This was the second Thursday that the babysitter had to leave early.

She was positive she was about to die.

There were three dogs and no gerbils.

She had never danced before, but how hard could it be?

The tea tasted like paint thinner.

She posted her profile and held her breath.

The beef was overcooked.

He was completely shocked.

This was no time for the toaster to start smoking.

It was a brand new laptop.

She looked good, and felt better.

The walls had recently been painted blue.

If he didn't hurry, he was going to miss the tip off.

She didn't normally fawn over actors, but he had her swooning like a teenager.

It may have been Saturday night, but that didn't make it date night.

Twilight settled around them without much fuss.

They sat in a circle, holding hands.

She had always dreamed about taking a trip to London.

He was very still, listening intently.

The knocking at the door was insistent.

Trouble seemed to follow her where ever she went.

Murder investigations didn't usually start out like that.

She had always thought he was the love of her life.

Some people were just superstitious.

Justice could be fleeting.

The dress was no longer fitting around the waist, and she wasn't sure why.

The beach was just too crowded for comfort.

There was no sign of a break-in, but the study had been ransacked.

She thought she never would get packed.

She waited alone in the doctor's office.

He'd always wanted children, but now he wasn't so sure.

For some people, changing their minds was as easy as changing their clothes.

It was far too early for that kind of racket.

Last Lines

And that is precisely why she never went fly fishing on a Monday.

So diamonds weren't always a girl's best friend?

He knew nothing would ever be the same again.

The lesson here, he decided, was that some people just couldn't be trusted.

October would always be his favorite month.

From now on, she would wear polish on her toes.

His brother's girlfriend had a lot to answer for.

The maid would have to be fired, after all.

She slammed the phone down.

He blew the whistle for the final time that afternoon.

The police arrived twenty minutes later.

It turned out that the soup was too salty after all.

Who knew she hated tomatoes that much?

He was never getting those stains out of the carpet.

Now she was going to have to get flood insurance.

Somehow, the hat stayed perched primly on her head.

He did always like a woman in uniform.

Momma always said nothing good happened after 10PM.

She still couldn't figure out why he shaved the dog.

She could always trust her sister to keep a secret.

Not every man could be a bull fighter.

If she never saw that squirrel again, it would be too soon.

Peanut butter and jelly had never been his favorite.

They would never know the truth, now.

Luckily, the couch ended up being on sale.

She knew they were going to get their happily ever after this time.

Someday she'd learn to stop eaves dropping.

It was the best decision he'd ever made.

Tomorrow would be another day.

The strawberry was, of course, the finishing touch.

The future was not something to be told, but aspired towards.

And to think, she missed her favorite TV show for this.

It seemed that love was more fun the second time around.

Sometimes he wished he drank.

Maybe she had a future as a private detective.

Maybe that would convince her that only a professional should cut her hair.

It was the most unusual wedding present ever.

They were just lucky the house hadn't caught on fire.

By the time it was over, no one was surprised he was guilty.

In the end, it wouldn't have mattered if they had gone or not.